The Shapes of Water

stories about patterns and shapes

Learning Media

CONTENTS

THE SHAPES OF WATER

BY GILLIAN SHANNON

When I was little, I loved water. I loved the way you could splash about with it, or let it trickle through your fingers. Water can change into so many different shapes.

Water can be very still and peaceful. It can also be spectacular when it falls as a waterfall or rushes along rivers after heavy rain.

Waves of seawater crash into the shore when it is stormy and can sometimes do quite a lot of damage.

There is water in the air too. We can see it when we look up at the clouds. Clouds are made of lots of tiny water droplets. Sometimes the water in the clouds falls to the earth as rain.

When the cloud is so low that we can walk through it, we call it **fog**. Fog can be quite spooky. You can often see it in river valleys.

If it is very cold in the clouds, the water droplets can freeze into ice crystals and fall as **snow**. Cold air can also make the puddles and ponds turn to **ice**.

It doesn't always snow when it's cold in the clouds. Sometimes raindrops form, get carried up by the wind to where it is even colder, and freeze. Then they fall as **hail**.

On some very cold mornings, you may wake up to a **frost**. The water on the ground has turned to ice. You can see the ice crystals on the leaves of these plants.

One of the most wonderful sights you can see is a **rainbow**. Rainbows form where sun shines through water droplets. You can make rainbows yourself by using the fine spray on a hose and watering the garden on a sunny day.

The Shapes of Leaves

by Gillian Shannon

Have you ever noticed how many different shapes of leaves there are?

Some plants, like grass, have long thin leaves; some, like the kiwifruit, have big round leaves. The leaves of the ice plant have water stored in them, so they are fat and squashy. Gorse has leaves shaped like spines to protect it from being eaten.

Rhubarb has a huge leaf. I once used a rhubarb leaf as an umbrella 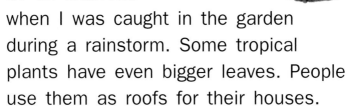 when I was caught in the garden during a rainstorm. Some tropical plants have even bigger leaves. People use them as roofs for their houses.

Plants make their own food from water, air, and sunlight. The place where this happens is inside the leaf. If you look closely at a leaf, you can see veins running through it. These veins carry water to the leaf, and take the food that has been made in the leaf to the rest of the plant.

15

Leaves not only have different shapes and sizes; they have different colors as well.

When I think of leaves, I always think of the color green because so many plants have green leaves. But not all leaves are green. Some plants have reddish leaves. Some have leaves with more than one color.

In the fall, the leaves of some plants change from green to red and gold. When they drop to the ground, they make a carpet of color. They are great to scrunch through when you are out walking. During winter, the leaves on the ground rot away. Then, in the spring, new leaves grow on the trees.

Next time you are in a garden, look carefully at the leaves. You will be surprised at just how many different shapes and colors you can find.

Hidden Seeds

by Gillian Shannon

When I was young, I was allowed to have my own garden. My parents gave me a packet of radish seeds to plant there. I didn't like the radishes that grew, but my brother did. He ate them all!

Most plants grow from seeds, but the seeds are not always easy to find. For a long time, I didn't know that the peas I ate at dinner were the seeds of the pea plant. When they are growing on the plant, peas are hidden inside a pod. When the pod dries out, it opens, and the seeds escape. Other seeds are hidden in pods too. The flax plant has a long black pod.

Some seeds are hidden inside fruit. An apple has seeds hidden in its core. The seeds grow after the apple has rotted away. Tomatoes also have seeds inside. So do bell peppers.

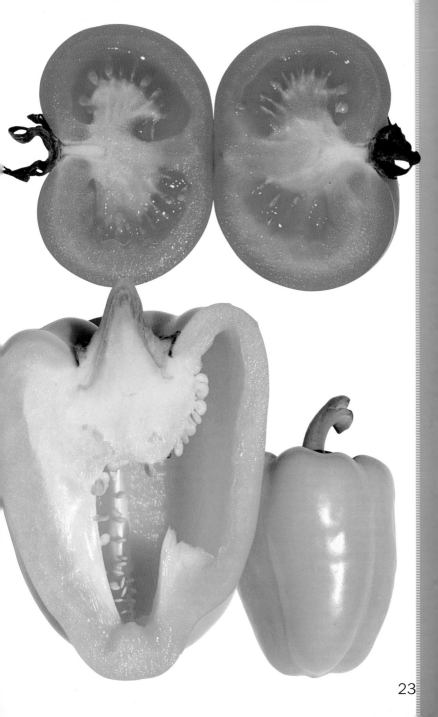

At Christmas, I like to buy walnuts to eat. Walnuts are large seeds. The part we eat is inside the hard shell. When the walnut begins to grow into a plant, it uses the nut as its food.

Rose hips also have seeds hiding inside. I remember my brother pushing these hairy seeds down my neck because they made me itch like *crazy*. I did not like the rose-hip time of year.

One of my favorite seeds is hidden inside a pine cone. As the cone opens, seeds drop out and float to the ground. Each seed has a tiny wing. If you find a pine cone which hasn't opened, keep it by a window in the sun. You can watch it open and see the seeds fall out.

Seeds come in all shapes and sizes –
and many of them are "hidden" seeds.
See how many different seeds you can
find.

Patterns from Fruit

by Clare Bowes

You will need:

an apple

thick paint

cardboard, paper, scissors, brushes, and a pencil.

1. Cut the apple in half, crossways. Look at the seed cases.

2. Draw a big picture of one seed case on a piece of card. Make your picture about four inches long. Cut it out.

3. Now draw a small circle in the center of a piece of paper.

4. Spread some thick paint over a piece of smooth cardboard.

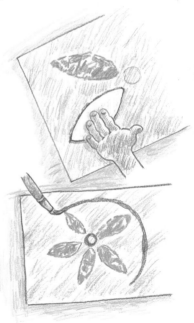

5. Press the piece of card (see step 2) into the paint. Lift it out and press it onto the paper, pointing out from the circle (see step 3). Do this five times, until you have a star shape.

6. Use a paint brush to decorate your design with other colors.

Now eat your fruit!

Other fruits have interesting patterns too. Cut open an orange or a pear to see what patterns you can find.

Leaf Patterns

by Clare Bowes

You will need:

some thin paint
an old toothbrush
pressed leaves
plain paper and newspaper.

1. Press some leaves. Put them between tissues or paper towels and put them under a big pile of books. Leave them overnight. In the morning, they should be flat.

2. Cover a table with newspaper. Put a pressed leaf onto a piece of plain paper.

3. Put some thin paint onto a plate and rub the toothbrush in it.

4. Hold the toothbrush over the leaf. Run your finger across the bristles.

5. Do this until there is plenty of paint splattered around the leaf.

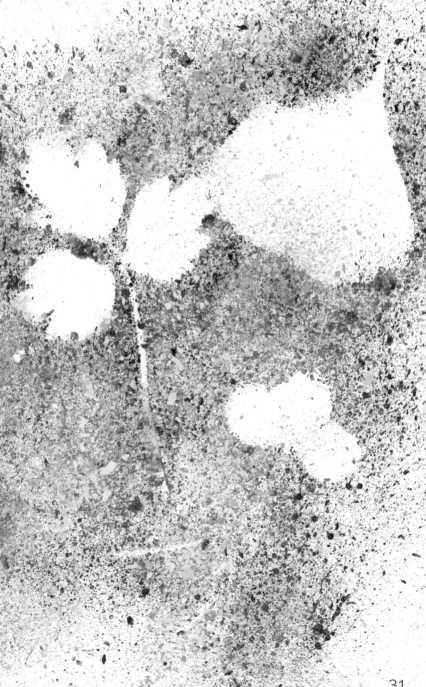